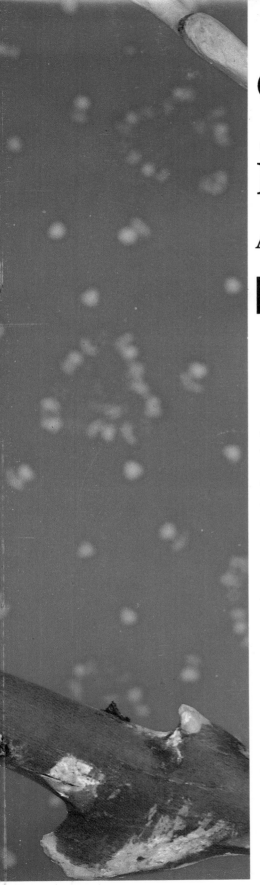

Can
...as a
Hobby

Anmarie Barrie

SAVE-OUR-PLANET SERIES

Distributed in the UNITED STATES to the Pet Trade by T.F.H. Publications, Inc., One T.F.H. Plaza, Neptune City, NJ 07753; distributed in the UNITED STATES to the Bookstore and Library Trade by National Book Network, Inc. 4720 Boston Way, Lanham MD 20706; in CANADA to the Pet Trade by H & L Pet Supplies Inc., 27 Kingston Crescent, Kitchener, Ontario N2B 2T6; Rolf C. Hagen Ltd., 3225 Sartelon Street, Montreal 382 Quebec; in CANADA to the Book Trade by Macmillan of Canada (A Division of Canada Publishing Corporation), 164 Commander Boulevard, Agincourt, Ontario M1S 3C7; in ENGLAND by T.F.H. Publications, PO Box 15, Waterlooville PO7 6BQ; in AUSTRALIA AND THE SOUTH PACIFIC by T.F.H. (Australia), Pty. Ltd., Box 149, Brookvale 2100 N.S.W., Australia; in NEW ZEALAND by Brooklands Aquarium Ltd., 5 McGiven Drive, New Plymouth, RD1 New Zealand; in the PHILIPPINES by Bio-Research, 5 Lippay Street, San Lorenzo Village, Makati, Rizal; in SOUTH AFRICA by Multipet Pty. Ltd., P.O. Box 35347, Northway, 4065, South Africa. Published by T.F.H. Publications, Inc. Manufactured in the United States of America by T.F.H. Publications, Inc.

Contents

Introduction

In 1478, the Spanish conquered Las Islas Canarias, a small group of islands located off the west coast of Morocco. These men could not have realized the dramatic effect this event would have on the little birds native to this land.

The birds of the species *Serinus canaria* were melodious. Shipped back to Spain, they became popular pets.

England refined and improved canary features to create the types seen today. Over 500 years later, these birds have developed into the

Intensive (opposite page) and non-intensive red factor canaries are just two of the many colorful canary strains available today. Photo by Michael Gilroy.

Initially, the shrewd Spanish sold only cock birds to other countries. Eventually, hens were acquired by the Italians. From that point on, breeders in Germany and

multifarious varieties of the domestic canary known and loved in homes around the world. Of course, the canary has changed considerably over the years. For example, the best singing canaries, the Rollers, are far superior to the original birds shipped from the Canary Islands.

Other birds, especially the Budgerigar, rival and surpass the canary's popularity in many countries. However, the canary easily remains the most popular cage bird in Spain. Many homes have several cages of these songsters.

Most people think of the canary as a yellow bird. However, the range of colors is from the original wild form to greens, blues, whites, cinnamons, pinks, grays, and reds. In addition, various feather markings, sizes, and shapes have been developed. The canary owner is all but spoiled for choice!

The canary was used by miners for centuries. They took these birds into the depths of the earth with them. When the canary stopped singing or died, the presence of gas was indicated. Since the canary was affected first, the

miners had advance warning of danger. It is not surprising that canaries became traditional favorites in mining communities. Workers became highly skilled at breeding these birds.

SCOPE OF THE HOBBY

Canaries are kept for many reasons, not the least of which is their beautiful song. People who live alone find them good company. The birds also give them something to look after. This fact has therapeutic value, particularly with the elderly. Many knowledgeable aviculturists gained their initial bird-keeping experience with canaries. Many have gone on to specialize in one of the canary varieties. Those with large display aviaries containing colorful finches invariably keep one or two canaries, both for their color and their song.

Today, as always, there is considerable interest in hybridizing canaries with other finches in order to

Variegated Border Fancy (left) and non-intensive gold Isabel canaries. Photo by Michael Gilroy.

The intensive yellow agate canary is not a strain popular with most casual hobbyists. Photo by Michael Gilroy.

obtain superb singing birds. The breeding of the New Color canaries is a more recent happening in the hobby. Happily, there produce a canary that will win honors at exhibitions.

Each of the afore-mentioned canary owners is interested in the shape and color of the birds he keeps. One highly specialized area of the hobby involves breeders concerned

are a number of people still interested in breeding and retaining some of the older canary varieties. Finally, there are those who continually strive to

only with song. The Roller is the ultimate songbird. Its followers are a dedicated group of enthusiasts.

The ancestral common canary (*Serinus canaria*) won't draw raves in the looks department, but what a songster! The upper bird is the male. Photo by Horst Bielfeld.

CLASSIFICATION

The canary is a member of a large group of birds known as the perching birds. Scientifically, the group is the order Passeriformes. The feet of perching birds have four toes: one lies backward, the other three forward. The order is divided into smaller groups known as families. Canaries are members of the family Carduelidae—the Carduelid Finches. Families are further divided into genera. The canary genus is *Serinus*. This genus contains some 32 species with a total of 71 subspecies among them.

Accommodations

Canaries can be kept in all types of avicultural housing. These types include aviaries, breeder cages, and the popular all-wire cages sold for pet birds. The accommodations should always be of the highest quality and the largest that you can afford. Settling for inferior housing is false economy.

AVIARIES

Flight aviaries are popular with just about all bird keepers. The major considerations of a good aviary are that it is well constructed, correctly situated, free from vermin, and easy to clean. Once these basics are established, esthetics may be considered. Generally, an aviary is attached to a fully enclosed structure. The shelter forms part of an even larger unit—the bird room. The caged stock, food, and equipment are kept in the bird room. This arrangement varies from a garden shed, with a single flight, through to a complete line of flights emerging from a very big bird room. This last is a costly and long-term project. It should be developed as experience grows, rather than attempted by a novice.

Everybody's idea of the typical canary—the intensive yellow Border Fancy. Photo by Michael Gilroy.

Large, walk-in outdoor aviaries are practical only in regions having mild year-round climates. Art by John R. Quinn.

Construction It is best to assemble aviary flights from individual frames of wood. The wood should be clad with welded wire of an approximate gauge of 19. The hole dimension is about 2.54 x 1.25cm (1 x 0.5 in). Treat the frames with a preservative, such as creosote, to prolong their life. Mixing the preservative with a bit of used motor oil adds to the life of the wood. Dry the treated wood thoroughly before birds are allowed near it. Bolt the frames together to form a rigid unit of the desired size. (Check on the available widths of welded wire before preparing the frames.) Resting the flight on a low cement or brick wall is attractive and provides a solid base for the frames.

Floor Concrete or paving slabs make the best aviary floors. They are both easy to clean, and they prevent mice, rats, and the like from burrowing under the wire frames. Incorporating a slight slope in the floor (away from the shelter) takes rainwater away.

Height A good flight height is 2m (6ft 6in).

This is above the average eye level, an esthetic consideration. The width and length are determined by space and money. A two-meter length by one-meter width is about the minimum for breeding flights.

Site This is an important consideration. However, the bird keeper is not always able to have his choice, due to space and zoning restrictions. If there is some choice, avoid situating the aviary under trees or on low ground. In addition, avoid northern and western exposures (avoid southern and eastern exposures in the southern hemisphere), where the birds are more exposed to cold winds and driving rain. If this cannot be avoided, then make some extra frames onto which clear or frosted plastic can be screwed. These frames can be bolted onto the exposed sides of the aviary during winter months. Likewise, similar panels covering one-third or one-half of the aviary roof enable the birds to sit outside, yet protected, even in the rain.

Fittings The only essential fixture in an aviary flight is a pair of perches running across the width. A perch at each end gives maximum flying

Smaller flights like this one are ideal as temporary, summer breeding enclosures. The wire netting has been omitted from these drawings in the interest of clarity. Art by John R. Quinn.

A view of a professional bird room, showing a bank of uniform, well-constructed breeding cages. Photo by Mervin F. Roberts.

distance between them. A large aviary can accommodate a shallow concrete bath. Those on pedestals look quite attractive. Nonpoisonous potted plants can be used

when the door is opened.

Access to Shelter The birds should enter the aviary shelter from the flight via a pop hole. One or more perches below the pop hole make a landing

for decoration. The plants should be removed periodically so that they have a time when the birds are not fouling them.

Safety Porch If space is available, a safety porch should be fitted in front of the aviary access door. This is an extra security feature. It minimizes the possibility of a bird escaping from an aviary

shelf. A pop hole which can be closed by a sliding door serves to keep the birds in the shelter during inclement weather.

The Shelter Canary shelters range from an indoor flight to a large stock cage. A shelter should have two perches, feeding pots, and a water container. It is useful for an indoor flight to have two doors—one for entry into the shelter and one from the shelter to the aviary. During warm periods, the latter door may be left open.

THE BIRD ROOM

A shelter within a larger structure doubles as a bird room. However, a bird room can be within your home if you have a spare room. It can also be a garage or shed not used for other purposes. The essentials of a bird room are good light, freedom from drafts and vermin, good ventilation, and good insulation. Avicultural periodicals have many articles covering design layouts for bird rooms.

A wooden structure is best raised about 30.5cm (12in) above ground level. This space provides under-floor ventilation and protection from vermin. Lining the building with plasterboard, chipboard, or the like helps keep it warm in the winter and cool in the summer. Some insulating material should be placed between the two walls. An electrical and a water supply are advantageous.

Temperature
Maintaining the correct temperature in the bird room is very important, yet it is often overlooked by novice breeders. These breeders then attribute failures to other causes, such as diet. Their attempts to adjust this by supplying additives only makes matters worse. Other breeders deliberately keep an unnaturally high temperature to encourage early breeding. They also increase the daylight hours with artificial light. Such measures are very short term because the vigor of the stock suffers.

Conversely, the theory that a cold bird room produces stronger chicks has little basis in reality.

A constant supply of fresh clean water is critical in the successful husbandry of canaries. These small dispensers are designed for easy removal and cleaning. Photo by Mervin F. Roberts.

Such birds use up much energy in just keeping warm at the very time their bodies need to channel all possible energy into their growth.

As with most things, the best course is the middle road. Birds must be protected from extremes. A good bird room temperature is regulated so that it does not fall below 4°C (39°F), nor rise above 32°C (90°F).

Lighting Fluorescent lights resembling natural sunlight are the best. Suddenly switching the lights on and off after dark can be quite distressing to canaries; the natural rhythm of the birds is upset. Dimmer switches and programmable timers are readily available these days; a suitable one should be acquired. A low-wattage bulb should be kept on overnight. In this way, startled canaries will not be injured because they cannot see to get back to their perch. A blue light is often favored for this purpose.

Air Fresheners Ionizers, which produce negative ions, are a recent development for bird rooms. These ions cling to dust particles, bacteria, and fungal spores. This unwanted material is rendered more harmless and is readily wiped away from the ionizer area. The air is freshened and respiratory problems are reduced. Ionizers are

Placement of an outdoor aviary is important: it should be sited where it will be partially shaded and not exposed to overly windy conditions. Art by John R. Quinn.

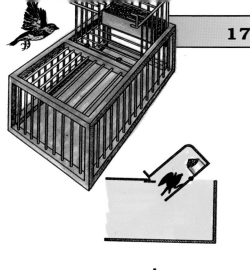

inexpensive
to purchase
and operate.

Storage Allow for
more storage space
and shelving than you
think necessary when
planning a bird room.
Extra cages, equipment,
books, and other items
rapidly multiply until space
is at a premium. Likewise,
it does not take many
matings before the seed
volume is dramatically
increased. It must all be
stored where it is safe from
vermin and protected from
moisture.

Windows Sunlight is
important to all birds. It is
needed in the production of
vitamins and for general
well being. Windows
should be covered on the
inside with fine mesh. This

allows them to be
open in warm
weather without the
birds being able to fly
out. It also keeps other
creatures from getting in.

Paint All surfaces must
be suitably painted for
protection and for ease of
cleaning. A light, cheerful
color enhances to the
surroundings. Paints can
be impregnated with
acaricides to keep the risk
of mite infection down.

CAGES

There are two types of
cages: those for pets and
those for breeders. We'll
begin with the latter first.

Breeder cages can be
made or purchased as
either single, double, or
triple breeders. The single

Above left:
Two nest box
designs that
allow the
breeders to
be
segregated
from the rest
of the flock.
Above right:
An ingenious
trap designed
to be placed
within an
aviary. The
problem: how
to target the
right bird!

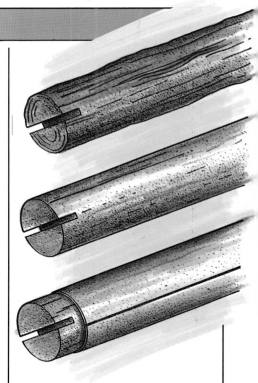

breeder is limited and costly in comparison. The other two offer more flexibility of use. Basically, a breeder cage is a box unit. The front is of all-wire construction. A strip at the bottom facilitates the removal of a wooden, metal, or plastic sand or sawdust tray. The cage size is governed by available space and funds. A double breeder, however, should be about 91 x 25.5 x 38cm (36 x 10 x 15in). A triple is about an extra 15.25cm (6in) in length.

The double breeder contains a sliding partition that divides the unit in two. The triple has two such dividers. The dividers are usually wire. In this way, birds can still see each other, and hens can feed their chicks. A useful-sized stock cage exists when the partitions are removed.

The triple breeder is useful if a cock is paired with two hens. He is placed in the central part. One partition is removed for him to mate with a hen.

Purchased breeder cages are typically unpainted. The usual combination of colors is black outside and white inside. A number of breeders nowadays use pastel colors inside. Wood preservatives are used to discourage parasites.

If you are a do-it-yourselfer, a single run of four or five double breeders decreases the overall cost per cage. An alternative to using plywood is to use a coated wood, such as melamine. This is easy to wipe clean, but it is heavier and more costly. Cage fronts can be purchased from pet stores or specialist bird traders.

Most cages include a pull-out floor tray for ease of cleaning. Some breeders do not use trays at all. In such cases, a hinged piece of wood prevents sand from spilling out. The dirty floor covering is simply swept out once the lip is lowered. Another variation is to have a removable cage front. It

can be on a frame or mounted so that it slides down between wooden or plastic channels.

Multiple cage units can be arranged in tiers. The tiers must be separated so that air can circulate between each row and around the back. Individual cages can be replaced on a rotational basis. Likewise, one can be repainted away from the bird room. A visit to a canary breeder yields ideas and

forestalls problems.

Perches Each cage needs two perches. They can be placed at the same or at differing heights at either end of the cage. This distance maximizes the birds' exercise. A very large

Tempers flare at a seed dish, clearly indicating that it is too small to accommodate two birds at once. Photo by Michael Gilroy.

cage can accommodate three, two at one height, and one midway but much higher. Make sure the perches are far enough from the sides of the cage so that tail feathers are not damaged from rubbing against the wires. Also, allow enough headroom clearance. Perches of varying thickness help exercise the birds' feet and legs. However, a perch that is too thick or too thin does not allow a proper grip. Softwood is preferred over hardwood.

Perches can be bought from a pet-supply store. However, a branch from a fruit tree can make a suitable perch. The birds will enjoy nibbling at the bark, twigs, and buds. Be sure, however, that none of the branches have been treated with poisonous chemicals.

Food Dishes Cages typically come with seed and water containers. However, plastic or ceramic dishes can be used as well. Place the dishes

on the floor of the cage away from the perches. This prevents the food from being contaminated by droppings. Some cages

An enclosed bird bath will help prevent the soaking and subsequent souring of the cage floor. Photo by Horst Bielfeld.

provide places for the dishes to be hung from the side of the cage. This avoids tipping and lessens the chance of droppings ending up in them. Such a cage is likely to have individual doors for each dish. These doors facilitate cleaning and refilling.

Canaries feed by cracking open seed. The shed hulls are often dropped back into the dish and accumulate on top of the remaining seed. Some birds cannot find the food underneath the hulls. Therefore, the husks must be blown off each day so the fresh seed can be found.

Seed hoppers can be used instead of open dishes. They have drawers that catch the hulls and can be emptied. These drawers, however, partially cover the seed. When a seed hopper is first introduced, be sure your birds are capable of finding the food. Check hoppers daily to be sure they are not clogged with seed.

Water A supply of fresh water must always be available. Without it, birds will die in 24 hours. The water can be supplied via open pots or gravity-flow bottles. These bottles keep the water clear of feces and seed husks. Clean and replenish the water

container every day.

Floor Coverings A variety of materials can be used for floor covering. Many breeders use sawdust. However, sawdust clings to the birds' feathers and scatters easily. Sand is an alternative, but it can stain the feathers of very light colored canaries. Newspaper print rubs off on the birds to make them look dirty. Paper towels or sheets of plastic work well. A layer of corn cob or the like can be used for extra absorbency. Some cages have a bottom grate which keeps the birds from contacting the cage floor. With a cage grate, sand or gravel paper can be used. The grate prevents the birds from eating soiled sand and becoming ill. Replace the cage litter every two or three days, or

Seed and water cups should be cleaned frequently to prevent disease. Photo by Dr. Herbert R. Axelrod.

whenever the mess makes you uncomfortable.

Baths All canaries enjoy bathing. Regular bathing also adds to the birds' cleanliness and appearance. A number of suitable bird baths can be purchased. They simply hang over an open cage door. Alternatively, canaries can be bathed with a fine mist of warm water from a spray bottle. Some owners like their birds to bathe in the kitchen sink. Others even bring a bird or two into the shower with them. These pets often fly to the sink or shower as soon as they hear the water running!

Pet Bird Cages The traditional type of cage for a pet canary is all wire. Select the largest one you can afford and accommodate. Length is the most important single consideration. Tall, circular cages are not suited to any bird species. A better choice for a cage is a double or triple breeder cage. This allows far more room in which to fly. Even better is an indoor flight that blends in with the room. Such pens can be very attractive.

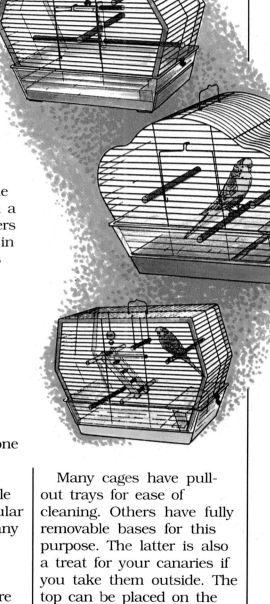

Many cages have pull-out trays for ease of cleaning. Others have fully removable bases for this purpose. The latter is also a treat for your canaries if you take them outside. The top can be placed on the grass to let them get a taste of nature! The cage normally comes with two perches and with food and water containers. If the perches are plastic, replace them with wooden dowels or natural branches.

Situation
Some all-wire cages come complete with stands. If the stand is not well weighted, do not bother with it. Such a stand can be tipped over rather easily. A good stand is specially weighted in its base.

The cage should be situated in a bright spot, yet protected from direct sunlight. The area should be free of drafts, so place the cage away from doors and windows. The cage should be placed at eye level since birds are intimidated by overhead movement. Placing the cage against a wall provides a sense of security for the bird. A corner spot is even better.

On nice days, a canary appreciates fresh air. A shaded spot on a porch is ideal. However, never leave your pet unsupervised when outdoors.

Cage Maintenance
Wash and dry the cage bottom weekly, and periodically wash the cage bars. Scrubbing with a stiff brush loosens any dried debris. Clean the perches with a brush, fine sand paper, or a perch scraper. Let them dry completely before placing them back in the cage. Wet or damp perches cause arthritis, rheumatism, and colds. The food and water dishes need to be washed daily with hot water and soap. During the thorough cleaning, you might like to have a smaller holding cage available for the birds.

A selection of popular cage styles. The ideal cage offers the occupant plenty of room for free movement.

Stock Selection

The first decision prospective canary owners make is which type of canary to keep. Generally, a pet owner's idea of a canary is met by the yellow varieties. These are attractive birds and are good singers. Additionally, they are the most readily available canaries in pet shops. Many of the other popular varieties are also nice singers.

An owner planning to breed and exhibit canaries should visit as many bird shows as possible to become familiar with the many varieties.

If you cannot decide which variety to breed, then start with a popular bird. Keep some of the lesser-

The selection of a pet canary involves the traditional principles: bright eyes, alert behavior, good appetite and healthy plumage. Photo by Michael Gilroy.

seen types to gain canary keeping experience. If a variety is not popular in your area, you could become a well-established breeder and supplier of this variety.

QUALITY BIRDS

Once you have fixed on the variety you wish to breed, view as many examples as possible. The pet shop is the first place

The variegated Border Fancy canary is one of the more popular cage bird pets. Photo by Michael Gilroy.

to visit; the dealer can tell you what varieties are available in your area. In addition, talk with breeders and judges. They will tell you what you should look for in a particular type.

The number-one priority in choosing any bird is health. No circumstance justifies purchasing an unhealthy canary as a pet or for breeding.

The cost of housing, feeding, and exhibiting poor birds is the same as for high-quality stock. Therefore, initially purchasing quality stock is more economically efficient in the long run. Good stock produces youngsters worth two or three times as much as inferior stock. Sound stock is also easier to sell.

TYPE

Type refers to the conformation of an animal. It must be well balanced, not exaggerated in any given area. Each canary variety has its own standard of excellence against which it is judged. Its type is the overall impression it gives in relation to that standard. A canary's quality is based on how well its individual components compare to those of other birds of the same variety. Birds of good type may not always be big show winners. However, they are the birds from which winners

are bred.

Breeding must be commenced with choice specimens exhibiting no major faults. It takes several generations just to get your stock up to breeding quality if you start with poor-quality birds. The novice breeder needs to place trust in a more experienced breeder for advice on stock selection.

THE BREEDER

There are a few pointers for selecting the right breeder when you are at a show. Someone who has won in a small class of five or six birds has not achieved the same success as a winner in a class of 20 or more birds. Some breeders consistently win with birds of outstanding merit. Yet, these same birds may be quite inept at passing on these qualities to future generations. A breeder with regular wins is preferable to one with an occasional high flyer. The chances are that the former birds are typical of the breeder's overall stock. In the latter case, there may be a lot of inferior birds in the stockroom. You must look for carefully bred

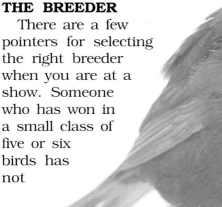

Investing in top-quality stock can help to ensure success in your breeding program.

Show quality or not, the red factor canary makes for a colorful, attractive pet! Photo by Michael Gilroy.

birds that are uniform for their type and that are known to pass on that type. The breeder's bird room is the place to visit to examine his entire stock. Overall, the stock should be almost as good as that which is exhibited.

It is unlikely that breeders will part with their best birds. You don't need their best anyway, only those of sound quality. Even with good birds, much still has to be done to produce winners. The thrill of success is then that much more exciting and rewarding.

AGE

Whether as a pet or for breeding, young birds are best. A hen's best breeding years are while she is less than three years old. A cock is useful for breeding into his sixth or seventh year. Young birds are easier to tame and train as pets.

COLORS

When choosing yellows, it is wise to have some variegated birds as well. Yellow-to-yellow matings do not steadily produce the best quality in this color. This example is typical of many colors, where the best birds are produced by introducing another color. Discuss this aspect with an experienced canary keeper, who will advise you as to why he selected birds you may have considered a mismatch.

SINGING QUALITY

The pet owner must purchase a cock bird if he wants a singing canary—female birds only chirp. If you plan to breed song canaries, then you should visit Roller canary exhibitions. These are not held in conjunction with regular bird shows. Roller canaries must be kept

away from other bird sounds which they might incorporate into their songs.

Rollers are judged entirely on their song—color is of secondary importance. Since Roller breeding is a specialized area of canaries, you should join the national society for these birds. However, membership in any canary variety club is strongly recommended. You meet new

friends with a common interest, and you also gain a lot of advice from

attending the regular club meetings. If you plan to exhibit, membership in the various clubs may be required.

Canaries relate well to each other, but a single bird is more easily tamed and trained. Photo by Michael Gilroy.

Canary Varieties

The traditional and the off-beat pose side-by-side: The Norwich (left) and Gloster canaries. Photo by Michael Gilroy.

In general, canary varieties have names that reflect the area in which they became popular. The canaries seen in the USA, the UK, and Australia are essentially birds developed in the different regions of Great Britain. The exception is the Roller canary, a bird of German origin. In more recent times, the USA has produced its own canary, the American Singer. Certain European canaries, such as the frilled types, have gained a small but growing following. This book reviews all of the popular varieties and some of the less-seen ones. There are many canary varieties that were popular in England at the turn of the century which are no longer around today. It is hoped that all of the present day varieties will have sufficient support to ensure their continuation.

TERMINOLOGY

There are a number of descriptive terms used for canaries. Those that are more common are discussed so that you may understand the terms when visiting shows and speaking with breeders.

Type Canaries: The shape is the most important factor when judging these canaries.

Examples are the Border and the Norwich.

Color Canaries: These canaries are bred for color. Many colors are available.

Pattern Canaries: The only surviving pattern canary is the Lizard. The feather markings are its only essential feature.

Although the varieties have a bias toward type, color, or pattern, other aspects are still important. For example, the Yorkshire is a bird of position, as are one or two other varieties. However, the head shape, size, and condition all score points toward the maximum 100 allocated in competition.

Ticked: A ticked bird has a dark mark about the size of a small coin. Instead of one mark, a bird may have three dark feathers on the wing or tail.

Variegated: These birds exhibit variable amounts of dark feather, more so than ticked birds. Variegated birds may be one of three kinds: (a) variegated—more light areas than dark; (b) heavily variegated—more dark feathers than light; or (c) three parts dark—75% dark.

Foul: This is the opposite of a ticked—light marks on a dark bird.

A blue-variegated white Yorkshire canary. A rather uncommon color variety.

Clear: There are no visible dark feathers on the bird.

Self: The opposite of a clear—this is a completely dark bird.

Frosted: The tips of the feathers lack pigment, giving a frosted appearance.

Buff: This term has the same meaning as frosted. However, it is coupled with the structure of the feather, which is larger and coarser than the normal feather of yellow canaries.

Crest: The ring of head feathers that fan out like a rosette around the crown.

Corona: The crest of a Gloster canary.

Plainhead: The head has normal, not crested, feathers.

Consort: This is

The red-factor is a classic example of the "color canary." Photo by Michael Gilroy.

a Gloster canary with no crest. Thus, it is a plainhead.

Cap: The crown on the head of a Lizard canary is a cap.

Flighted: A bird over one year old on which all the feathers have been molted.

Unflighted: A bird under one year old on which only body feathers have molted. Those of the wing and tail are retained until the next molt.

Close- or closed-rung: A bird carrying a closed metal ring, or band, on its leg. These rings serve as permanent means of identification of the bird. They are not compulsory in exhibition canaries, although they are recommended. They are required in exhibition Roller canaries.

Open rung: An open rung bird carries a split ring of metal or plastic on its leg. These rings can be put on or taken off at any time. They are a useful means of temporary identification.

THE BORDER FANCY CANARY

Maximum size: 14cm (5.5in). This is one of the most popular of all canary varieties, from both the standpoint of the pet owner and the breeder-exhibitor. The Border Fancy canary is recommended for beginners. However, its exhibition standard is extremely high. A trio of good Borders is reasonably priced, but high quality stock may command large sums. This variety, developed in the English-Scottish border lands, was formerly the smallest of canaries. It was originally known as the Cumberland, an old county name in northern England. In

A beautiful yellow Border Fancy canary—the classic "yellow bird" of the pet trade. Photo by Michael Gilroy.

The variegated Norwich canary, one of the oldest of canary strains. Photo by Michael Gilroy.

When selecting a canary, the bird's overall health should be your prime consideration. Photo by Michael Gilroy.

THE NORWICH CANARY

Maximum size: 16cm (6.5in). The Norwich canary is one of the oldest canary breeds, dating back to the 1850s. It is a large canary with a relatively short, cobby body. The neck is short and thick. The tail is short. The legs are placed well back under the body. These birds are often described as sluggish, but this is misleading. The standard calls for "bold and bouncing movement." These big canaries do not hop about like Borders or Glosters; this does not imply, however, that they are sluggish.

The Norwich is well supported at exhibitions. Good ones can take supreme awards. However, you need to be dedicated, because this variety has a high percentage of very experienced fanciers. Once out of the novice class, the real challenge begins!

THE YORKSHIRE CANARY

Size: 17cm (6.75in). This is another old breed, dating back to the latter part of the 19th century. The Yorkshire canary is quite large. It is often called "the gentleman of the fancy" due to its elegant, upright stance. It is very much a bird of position. Along with quality of feather, position accounts

A cinnamon variegated Yorkshire canary.

for half of the 100 points allocated to the exhibition bird. The Yorkshire has changed considerably over the years. It is now a bulkier bird, being wedge-shaped rather than slim. Therefore, it is now easier to obtain large birds than it was in the past.

The Yorkshire is available in all the normal canary colors. It is also a color-fed variety. Long legs are important in a good Yorkshire. So, too, is the length of the tail. It must be carried in a straight line with the body to give a soldier-like appearance. Show birds are bathed. It is advisable for an experienced fancier to show a beginner this technique.

THE LIZARD CANARY

Size: 12cm (4.75in). The Lizard canary is the oldest of all the canary varieties. It is the only one in which the pattern on the feathers is the most important aspect of the exhibition bird. At one time there was another patterned canary, the London Fancy. This variety died out shortly after the First World War. The Lizard almost became

in shape. The official standard makes no reference to this or to size. The markings are all-important, regardless of any other feature. These marks, called spangles, should be distinct rows going down the body. The rows should enlarge as they approach the tail. The spangles are larger on the back and wings than on the underside. Thus the

A green Lizard canary has a feather to pick with a cagemate. Photo by Michael Gilroy.

extinct at the end of World War II. Only a handful existed then.

The Lizard is one of the few canaries not named after a locality. Instead, it is named for the scale-like feather markings that resemble those of a lizard.

The Lizard is somewhat like a slim Border canary

underside appears darker. This uniformity and distribution of the spangles account for 25 of the 100 show points. The feathers must be tight, fitting to the body. They must have a smooth, silky quality.

The cap of a Lizard may be clear or marked with dark feathers.

THE FIFE FANCY CANARY

Maximum size: 11.5cm (4.5in). The Fife Fancy canary, named for the area in Scotland, is the most recent variety. It is a miniature Border canary, a direct result of the fashion among Border breeders for size. A number of long-standing Border enthusiasts, concerned with the growing tendency for large Borders, preserved the original "wee gems." So was born the Fife Fancy in 1957.

In the next decade or so, progress in the variety was slow and localized to Scotland. However, the Fife Fancy is seen in many British shows. It attracts rather large entries. Over 300 birds are on display in some shows. The Fife is an

excellent choice for those looking for a small, appealing canary with a good turn of song. It can be regarded in all ways as a Border canary.

Intensive gold Isabel canary. Photo by Michael Gilroy.

The Gloster Corona resembles a Crested Canary but is smaller and less heavily feathered. Photo by Michael Gilroy.

THE CRESTED CANARY

Size: 18.5cm (7.25in). At its peak of popularity, the Crested canary was known as the Turncrown. The Crested has been used in many varieties to establish more size, but not always without side-effects. The Crested is a large bird, sporting a full crest extending over the eyes. It resembles the Norwich. It is more heavily feathered, however, than the latter. Crested birds are not paired together due to a lethal factor. A Crested is bred to a Plainhead, termed a Crestbred.

These birds once commanded high prices. They are rarely seen today, however. A true Crested canary is difficult to find; ask your pet dealer if he can locate one for you. If not, a letter to your national cage-bird magazine is the answer. If not for the Old Varieties Canary Association in the UK, the Crested might have died out altogether. This association was specifically formed to preserve such varieties.

THE LANCASHIRE COPPY CANARY

Size: Over 17.75cm (7in). The Lancashire is the largest of the canary varieties. It was once extremely popular—especially in the north of England, where it originated. The rigid standards and high prices had a negative effect on popularity. Experienced breeders dominated the field. The younger breeders established themselves in newer varieties. Some varieties survived these trends while others did not.

This is another of the old varieties that may have died out if not for the Old Varieties Canary Association. In fact, the Lancashire did die out but was re-established. The OVCA encouraged selective breeding of other canaries which had received gene infusions from the Lancashire. Although the present-day type may not equal the Lancashire of yesteryear, the resemblance is striking. Today's variety is aptly known as the Lancashire Coppy. It combines size with good looks. This variety is not common in most pet shops, although a pet dealer may be able to order one for you.

The crest is not completely round as it is in the Crested canary; it is of a horseshoe shape. The open end is to the rear of the head. Here the feathers should merge with those of the neck. In profile, the bird should be full chested, tapering to the tip of the tail.

This Gloster corona canary looks much like a sparrow with a Beatle-cut! This is one of the older canary strains. Photo by Horst Bielfeld.

CINNAMON CANARY

Size: 16cm (6.25in). The Cinnamon canary is another old variety. Although not enjoying its former popularity, it is still found in good numbers. The Cinnamon is similar in shape to the Norwich. Indeed, it would be grouped with the one-third of the total 100 exhibition points. The yellow must show no movement toward green. The striping of the back should be faint.

The variegated Border Fancy canary. Photo by Michael Gilroy.

Norwich if there were no separate classification for it at a show.

As the name implies, color is the major feature. It commands just over Cinnamon is found in all canary varieties; it is often used by breeders to improve the quality of feather in their stock. This variety does not appeal to the average pet owner.

BELGIAN AND SCOTCH FANCY CANARIES

Size: 17cm (6in). These varieties are similar in many ways. Both adopt unusual show positions compared to the average exhibition canaries. The Belgian canary retains a straight back and tail stance. The neck is stretched forward and the bird looks down to the floor. The Scotch Fancy stands such that it forms a half circle, the back gently bending and the tail sweeping under the perch. Actually, the overall profile resembles a half oval.

The stance of these birds scores 25 points. Another 20 points for shape is vital. It is essential that these canaries receive a lot of cage training. The birds do not stand in this exaggerated position without training. Of course, they must have inherited a predisposition to do this. Color is not important in these varieties. They must possess neat, tight fitting feathers and a small head, though.

The Scotch Fancy increases its followers every year in the UK. Virtually extinct at one time, it was taken under the supervision of the OVCA. The Belgian Fancy, one of the very oldest varieties, is less popular. It maintains a few dedicated enthusiasts, though.

The Scotch Fancy canary adopts its odd stance only after much training. This is not a commonly seen bird in the U.S. Photo by Harry V. Lacey.

FRILLED CANARIES

It is generally thought that the original Frilled canaries were developed in Holland during the 1700s. Today there are many varieties named after countries and cities. There are the Dutch, Parisian, Milan, Gibber Italicus, Spanish, Padovan and more. Some of these varieties are attractive while others are grotesque. Essentially, these birds are named for the way in which the back, chest and thighs carry curled feathers. These feathers are termed the mantle, jabot, and fins, respectively.

Frills are found in all colors. Good qualities of type in one variety are considered negatives in another. If the more unusual appeals to you, then Frilled varieties may be for you. Some traveling may have to be done to obtain good pairs of them. Prices will not be cheap.

The Frilled canary appeals to the interest in novelty. It is not an overly hardy strain. Photo by Michael Gilroy.

NEW COLORED CANARIES

Maximum Size: 12.75cm (5in). The keeping and breeding of the New Colored canaries are the most rapidly expanding areas of the fancy. Show entries are increasing steadily all of the time.

introduction of red genes from the Red Siskin, *Carduelis cucullata*, of Columbia and Venezuela, that really put the bang into the New Colors. Dr. Duncker of

The red factor canary is one of the more popular of the colored canaries. The color red in canaries is the result of both gene action and feeding. Photo by Michael Gilroy.

Although breeding for color has been evident for many years, it has gathered momentum with the growing number of mutations and re-combinations of these.

The earliest canary color mutations were the dominant white and the cinnamon. It was the

Germany produced fertile siskin x canary hybrids. A. K. Gill of the UK bred the first British red-factor canaries. Further mutations followed. By the

Exposure to sunlight may result in the bleaching out of color in a red factor canary. Photo by Michael Gilroy.

1950s, interest really began to show.

The term *red-factor* denotes birds carrying siskin genes. *New Colored* is applied to the colors now transferred to other canaries and the mutations since occurring from these. Numerous specialty clubs are now devoted to the various colors.

These birds were initially allocated 75 points for their color. Type began to suffer badly, though. Now only 55 points are given for color and 30 are given to overall shape. New Colored canaries are not type birds in the same way as are the Gloster and Norwich canaries. Even so, they have their own qualities. They are somewhere between a wild canary and a Border— without the roundness of the latter.

Color feeding is standard with these birds. Understand, though, that no amount of color feeding puts a color into a bird if it is not already present. Likewise, the brassy green or overly dark coloration seen in these birds is not thought to be the result of too much color feeding. Color in these birds is of a polygenic nature; numerous genes interact to produce a given effect. This is then affected by food; certain vegetables encourage redness while others encourage yellow pigment formation. Exposure to sunlight during molting may result in a diluting or bleaching effect on the newly emerging plumage. This means that there will always be considerable variation of color between individuals, including those of the same clutch. It takes years of experimentation to determine the right balance to obtain a given effect. Even then the colors are subject to continuous variation; transmission of dark and other factors is a matter of random combination.

canary of good type and superb song. The result was the combination of a Roller canary (69%) and a Border canary (31%).

The American Singer is judged against its own standard. It differs from the Roller in delivering its song while perched. The Roller sings on the move or when perched. Because of

The American Singer canary lacks the musical repertoire of the Roller but nonetheless makes a fine songster and pet. Photo by Michael Gilroy.

AMERICAN SINGER CANARY

Maximum Size: 14.6cm (5.75in). The American Singer canary is a relative newcomer, and it becomes more popular with each passing year. This variety was developed to meet the needs of those wanting a the need to consider type, the American Singer is always a

COLUMBUS FANCY CANARY
Size: 14.6cm (5.75in). This is a crested bird with a plainhead equivalent. The key feature of the Columbus Fancy is the crest. Type is being improved upon steadily.

Numerous British varieties were used in the initial development.

com-promise. It cannot match the Roller for song, nor can it best a good Border for type. It is an excellent all-around bird and a super pet, though.

ROLLER CANARY
Size: 12cm (4.75in). The average canary has a pleasant song. Compared to a top Roller canary, though, it is only an amateur. The Roller is a bird apart from all the others. It has been bred exclusively for the quality of its song for over 200 years. The origins of the Roller are found in the area of St. Andreasburg in the Harz Mountains of Germany. Four hundred families are believed responsible for the breeding and training of these birds. Various machines and assorted contraptions were made to produce sounds that were like water flowing over rocks. The Roller learned to

imitate these sounds. Nightingales also were used in the development of the Roller's song. The name is derived from the rolling way in which the bird delivers its song.

There are thirteen passages in the Roller's song repertoire. These are termed *rolls* and *tours.* Many have German names which are used internationally. Examples are the Glucke tour, Koller tour and Schockel. Others terms are English, such as the hollow roll and flutes. The training of a Roller is a highly developed art. These days recordings are used. There are trainers, though, who adhere to the time-tested method of using first-class birds as tutors to young birds.

Neither type nor color is of importance to a good Roller. However, there are a number of colors from which to choose. It was once stated that the greener the bird, the better the song. The fact is, however, that

Opposite page: Natural wood perches are always better for most cage birds. This canary is busy investigating a hunk of bogwood. Photo by Michael Gilroy. **Left:** The Roller canary may be seen in a wide variety of colors, from bright yellow to variegated to green or red. Photo by Michael Gilroy.

variegated yellows gained top awards in the 1950s, showing that this is not always so. Apart from greens, there are whites, blues, fawns and orange, as well as variegations of varying amounts. In recent years, there has been an effort to produce lighter colored birds. These appeal more to pet owners. If you admire good singing quality, then purchase on this basis alone. Forget what the bird looks like.

It is essential to stick to one strain when breeding Rollers. This maxim is applicable to any canary variety. The mixing of genes has little to recommend it in this case. If someone has developed the song of their canaries over the years, build onto this. It saves you a lot of hard work.

Rollers are not exhibited with other canary varieties. They must not be placed where their talent for mimicry might pick up inferior notes of the normal canary or other birds. The Roller devotees are a specialized group of fanciers. They keep very much to themselves. Therefore, join your nearest Roller canary club if you take up this variety.

Competition Rollers are closed-rung.

CANARY HYBRIDS

Breeding canaries with other species has been in evidence for many years. It continues to attract a strong following in every generation. The fact that most of such crosses are sterile does not put people off. Indeed, it seems to act as a spur for renewed effort. Much of the fascination stems from the thrill of the unexpected. Add to this the possibility of establishing fertile hybrids. An example of hybridization is the canary x Red Siskin.

Some of the birds with which canaries are paired are the Greenfinch, Bullfinch, Linnet, Siskin and Goldfinch. Note that it is illegal to take birds from the wild in the UK, USA and many other countries. The only indigenous species that may be used are those bred in captivity and carrying closed rings.

OTHER CANARIES

There are many other canary varieties found in different countries under their local names. More than any other domesticated bird species, canary fanciers are great experimenters continually striving to create a new variety.

The color red in a canary is thought to indicate the presence of wild siskin genes. Photo by Michael Gilroy.

Feeding

Untying knots is not one of a canary's talents, but one gets the feeling these two may try it to get at the seed in the bag! Photo by Michael Gilroy.

No two breeders feed their stock in quite the same manner. Each develops a regimen that he is convinced is superior to that of his fellow breeders. Do not be surprised, therefore, if you are told you are feeding your canaries the wrong diet! If you follow the basic advice given here, there will be nothing wrong with the diet. Other comments are merely opinions. If you are lucky enough to get the advice of a seasoned champion breeder, listen to what he says. It has obviously served him well over the years. It is not beneficial to change diets every time someone professes to know all about feeding canaries, though.

Excess is stored as fat for use in keeping warm. The second seed type provides birds with proteins

BASIC DIET

The most basic diet is composed of plain canary seed, a small amount of rape or a seed of similar nutritional content, and water. On such a regimen, a canary will be kept alive and in reasonably good health. The mere basics, though, are not, by themselves, the recommended diet. However, let's consider why the basic diet achieves its objective.

Two major types of seed are available to your birds: those rich in carbohydrates and those rich in fatty oils and protein: The former provide energy to generate muscular action.

used to replace tissue worn out by the action of the muscles. Both types of seed contain minerals. The body requires minerals to

Perfectly adequate canary mixes are available at your pet or bird store.

A hungry intensive yellow canary investigates the possibilities in a spray of berries. Photo by Michael Gilroy.

produce good bone, help metabolic processes and to fight off disease.

ADDITIONS TO THE DIET

Both pet owners and breeders want their birds to thrive, not just to survive.

Therefore,

pine nuts, maw, and rape. Any of these can be substituted for plain canary seed and rape, providing birds will accept them. Some seeds are too large, while others may be

Above: Canaries investigate a large, tough seed head for edibles. Photo by Michael Gilroy.
Opposite page: Greens are especially rich in vitamins. Photo by Michael Gilroy.

additions beneficial to the basic diet must be considered. In the wild, canaries partake of various greenfoods and insects. They also peck on the ground and swallow small particles of grit. Furthermore, they are not restricted to one type of seed. From all of this we see that diversity leads to healthy birds.

Seeds such as wheat, maize, the millets, and canary seed are rich in carbohydrates. On the other hand, the proportion of proteins and fats is greater in linseed, sunflower, peanuts, hemp,

ignored. Therefore, the choice of canary seed and rape are traditional, based on years of feeding by experienced fanciers. Some birds readily take maw or niger, while others show little interest. Experiment to see what your birds favor.

Too many rich protein seeds or canary seed in the diet result in obese canaries. A ratio of four parts canary seed to one part protein seed is about the right proportion.

It is advantageous for your birds to accept a range of seeds. To a large degree, this is dictated by the tastes they acquire as youngsters. Adult canaries can be quite finicky over seeds they have not tasted previously. Thus, much depends on what the rearing hen prefers. Coax your stock to take variety. This in turn increases the chance that newly hatched chicks will do likewise.

Soaked Seed Birds enjoy soaked seed. To obtain soaked seed, simply place seed in water for 24 hours. Rinse it thoroughly and feed it to your stock.

A nonintensive gold Isabel canary. Greenfoods should be fresh and free of mold. Photo by Michael Gilroy.

Soaked seed is nutritious due to the chemical changes which begin to take place inside the seed.

Germinated Seed The protein and vitamin content rises dramatically when seed is permitted to germinate. Most birds are partial to seed in this form, especially when hens have chicks in the nest.

Any type of seed can be germinated. First, soak it in water for 24 hours. Rinse the seed and place it on a tray covered with paper towels. Set the tray in a warm, dark cupboard. Keep the towels moist. Small shoots should appear in 24 to 36 hours. Wash, rinse and feed the sprouts to the birds. If the seed fails to germinate, quality is lacking. It is a good idea to periodically germinate seed to test its freshness, particularly if you buy in bulk.

The seeding heads of grasses and wild plants are enjoyed by canaries. However, beware of collecting grasses from areas subject to chemical spraying, fouling by animals and contamination from exhaust fumes.

GREENFOODS

Greenfoods are especially rich in vitamins, which are vital to the healthy growth of birds. They fulfill many roles in the body, ranging from the prevention of disease to assisting in the functioning of vital organs. Excess vitamins are expelled in many cases. However, in some instances they are absorbed into the tissue and create imbalances. This is why there is no need to administer vitamin supplements if your stock takes in a good range of greenfood.

Variety again is recommended because certain greenfoods have a laxative effect. Others are astringent in their effect.

By supplying a variety, the plants balance one another. Spinach, cress,

Brussels sprouts and cabbage are excellent choices. Lettuce is well

A sprig of broccoli is avidly picked over by this duo of canaries. Photo by Michael Gilroy.

received although it has little nutritional value. Wild plants, such as chickweed and dandelion, are good selections. The entire plant, including the roots, can be offered after it has been washed and shaken. Plantain, nettle, clover and sowthistle are examples of the variety of wild plants. Plants can be laid on the cage floor or clipped to the cage wire with a clothespin. Any berries that wild birds eat are suitable for canaries.

Fruits, such as apple, raspberry and orange, can be offered along with root vegetables, such as carrot. Cut them up into little pieces and offer as a mixed salad.

Larger pieces of fruit or vegetable can be wedged between the cage bars for your pets to enjoy.

Carrot is especially beneficial to color-fed canaries. The carotene gives color to the feathers if fed during the molt. It is useful even after the molt since some feathers are continually lost and replaced. Therefore, a coloring agent gives the new feathers the desired color.

PROTEINS

In the wild, canaries eat the grubs of insects and similar organisms. Animal protein contains certain amino acids deficient in plants. Hence, it is desirable to include various proteins in the diet. There is no need to go out catching insects!

Fortunately, there are some excellent commercial softfood mixes and chick-rearing foods on the market. In fact, those prepared for canaries are sought after by other finch breeders and owners of softbilled birds and parrots.

You can prepare your own softfood mix. The essentials are usually bread crumbs or crushed biscuits, a mashed boiled egg, ground rice and possibly a seed, such as maw. The combination is moistened with warm gravy stock or milk and mixed well. Some breeders add sugar, others honey. Softfood is essential for hens rearing chicks. It is also useful as a tonic

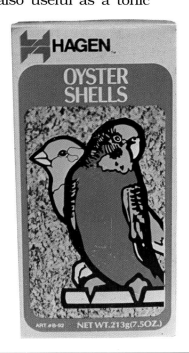

throughout the year, say once every ten days in small amounts. Any uneaten mix should be removed at the end of the day; it quickly sours.

GRIT AND CALCIUM

Canaries dehull their seed before swallowing it. Once ingested, the seed is not chewed in any way with their beak. The seed is ground up in the gizzard. To aid in this activity, particles of grit reduce the seed to a creamy consistency. It is thus important that your canaries are supplied with grit. This always should be available to them in a small pot. The size of the grit is also important. Tell your pet shop that it is for canaries.

The minerals required by a bird are normally met by the seed and other foods. However, one mineral is needed in quite large amounts. This is calcium. It is essential in the formation of good bones and strong eggshells. A lack of calcium results in poor bodies and soft-shelled eggs. Calcium is supplied via cuttlefish bone attached to the cage bars.

COLOR FEEDING

It is standard in New Colored canaries and the Norwich, Yorkshire and

Opposite page: Most berries that wild birds eat are safe for canaries. Photo by Michael Gilroy. **Left:** Oyster shells are a good source of calcium.

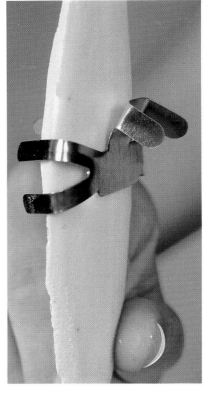

Years ago it was acceptable to color-feed canaries hot cayenne pepper. This is a rather cruel and drastic method. Numerous coloring agents are available from pet shops, specialty avicultural suppliers and seed merchants. Although some coloring agents are added to the drinking water, this can be messy. The birds splash the water over the cage and stain everything. This method is also unreliable in terms of dosage. Mixing the agent in with softfood is the better method.

Color feeding is a much debated aspect of bird keeping. Opinions differ greatly on how it best can be done to achieve the greatest effect. There are a few

Lizard varieties to supply a coloring agent during the molt. The color is passed into the newly growing feathers. The color feeding must commence prior to the molt so that the coloring agent is in the blood at the time the old feathers are shed. Color feeding must continue after the molt is complete; there are always a few later-developing feathers. If the birds are exhibited, color-feed them at least once per week throughout the show season.

general points to consider. Remember that no amount of color feeding puts good color into a bird lacking color in the first place. Next, blood, and therefore the feather, is limited in the amount of coloring agent it can contain. Overuse of the agent has no benefit. The quality of feather also affects the absorption rate of the agent. It is possible that the mental state of the bird has some bearing on the matter; the rate of molt is influenced by the mental state of the bird. A stressed bird almost certainly ends up with

patchy coloring. This is because the chemical state within its metabolism varies from that of the unstressed bird. Diet likewise affects coloring; certain seeds influence yellowness, others less so. In all cases the staining agent within foods is present in the blood and passed to the feathers. Color feeding is a more complex subject than is often believed by the novice. Experience with your own stock determines both the amounts of agent to be added, its frequency and the likely effect.

Above: Spray millet lends variety to the canary diet. Photo by Vince Serbin. **Below:** A large collection means lots of food. Always store seed and grit in clean, dry containers. Photo by Fred Harris.

FEEDING REGIMEN

Wild finches eat at different times of the day. Some are more active at midday, others earlier or later. Most birds in temperate climates do not have far to travel to their feeding grounds. This is so in the case of the wild canary. The wild canary commences feeding at dawn and continues throughout the day as opportunity affords.

Captive stock should have food available to them at all times. In this way they can feed whenever they are so inclined. Special treats, such as protein seeds, can be given each morning or evening. Treats can be alternated with greenfood. Softfood is best given early in the day and removed at lunch time. The most important thing to remember is that birds become accustomed to a fixed routine. Fix your times and stick to them.

Canaries tend to snack whenever they are hungry, at odd times of the day. Photo by Michael Gilroy.

Breeding

Canary breeding is a fascinating hobby. The novice breeder, though, is advised to solicit the help of an experienced breeder. Time and again, problems crop up that require the expertise of a trained breeder. Also, the novice quickly benefits from the experience the expert gained over many years.

BREEDING CONDITION

The predominant source of breeding failures and subsequent problems is that many breeders hurry their birds into breeding before they are

in proper condition. People induce birds to pair early because they want the youngsters through the molt for the coming show season. This is a short-sighted policy. It means that you are breeding to meet deadlines; quality is compromised

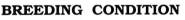

"Feed me! Feed me!" This hard-working hen seems to be taking a breather during the endless chore of feeding her growing young.

quickly. The care of the birds is what breeding is all about. The exhibition should be the highlight of displaying what you have produced—not the reason you produced it. In the northern hemi-sphere, canaries come into breeding

together.

With aviary birds, watch the weather to judge if the spring is true. Sometimes a warm period in early March is followed by bad weather later in the month and into April.

Stock that is well exercised over the winter should be of the right weight. The cocks bounce about and sing well. The hens indicate their readiness to mate by parading with a piece of grass or similar material

"When are you ever going to get around to building us a decent nest?" Photo by Michael Gilroy.

condition about April or as late as May. This gives them the advantage of increasing daylight hours in which to feed their young. In addition, frosty nights are less likely. Prepare the birds with this in mind. Do not set deadlines; let the birds indicate when they are ready. This means that not all birds will be ready

in their beaks. Such birds are ready to breed. Give the birds small amounts of softfood a week or two prior to their pairing.

PAIRING THE BIRDS

Canaries can be bred in two ways: one pair per breeding cage or two hens to one cock. In the former instance, leave the cock in with the hen to attend to all duties. In the latter, place the cock in the central cage of a triple breeder. Give him access to each hen in turn. Remove him altogether after mating.

Compatibility There is likely to be a lot of quarreling if a cock and hen

NEST PANS AND BOXES
Numerous nest pans and boxes are available. Nest boxes are typically made of wood. Some nest pans are fashioned from metal, others from plastic. Fix them firmly to

A clutch of canary eggs reposes in a nesting cup. This nest has been lined with a variety of materials, including grass, hair, and yarn. Photo by Harry V. Lacey.

are simply thrust together without introduction. Overcome this by placing a divider between them—one through which they can see each other and the cock can feed the hen. When the hen accepts food from the cock, remove the partition. If the hen ignores the cock through the divider, then she is not in breeding condition or she does not fancy your choice.

the back or side of the breeding cage. Place them when the hen is initially put in the breeding cage. The nest pan can be lined with a soft material like felt.

NEST BUILDING
Nest building begins in earnest once the pair are together. Canaries vary somewhat in this ability.

crucial developmental stage for the youngsters. Soaked seed, sprouted seed and high-protein seeds with a drop of cod-liver oil are appreciated.

FEATHER-PICKING HEN

Occasionally, a hen develops the bad habit of plucking her chicks. If the cock is not available to take over the feeding of these chicks, the best alternative is to place them in an adjoining cage. Then the hen can feed her young through the wires. If the hen is in a single breeder, place the chicks in a nursery cage hung in front of her cage. A nursery cage is simply a small cage.

SECOND ROUND OF EGGS

Even before the first round of chicks is ready to leave the nest, a fit hen wants to lay a second round of eggs. She may attempt nest building or repair while the first chicks are still in the nest. This typically happens around the 16th day or so. Be ready to forestall problems. Prepare a second nest pan to be placed in the cage. Move the nest pan with the chicks in it to another spot in the cage. The hen then settles down to lay her next round while the cock feeds the first round youngsters. If the hen plucks the feathers of the first chicks, place them and their father away from her. If a hen is a habitual plucker, withdraw her from the stud regardless of her quality.

Should the first round of eggs be infertile, the second round is usually more successful. Although

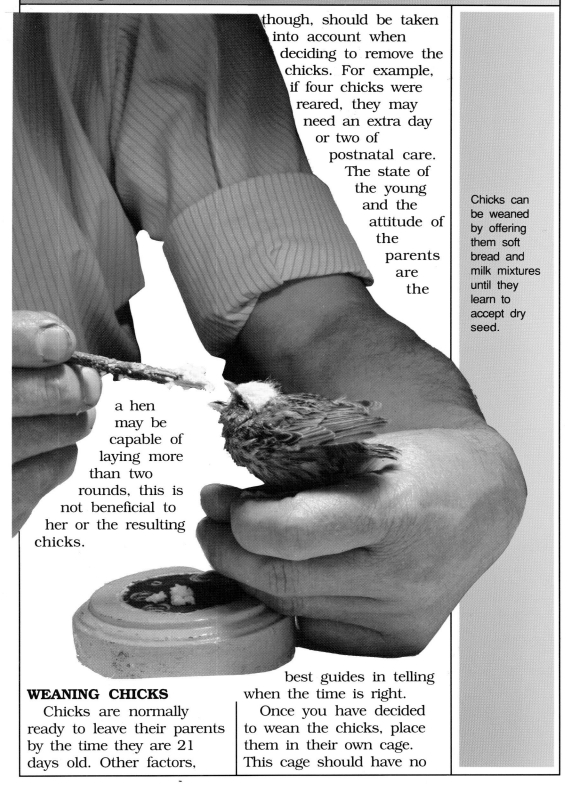

though, should be taken into account when deciding to remove the chicks. For example, if four chicks were reared, they may need an extra day or two of postnatal care. The state of the young and the attitude of the parents are the

Chicks can be weaned by offering them soft bread and milk mixtures until they learn to accept dry seed.

a hen may be capable of laying more than two rounds, this is not beneficial to her or the resulting chicks.

WEANING CHICKS

Chicks are normally ready to leave their parents by the time they are 21 days old. Other factors,

best guides in telling when the time is right.

Once you have decided to wean the chicks, place them in their own cage. This cage should have no

Canary chicks put on size quickly if fed well. Shown here are six-day-old chicks. Photo by Ron Moat.

perches and a floor covering of paper. Place seed in containers and scatter it on the floor. Provide softfood, including bread and milk, three times a day on a decreasing basis over three weeks. Soaked milk bread can have seed sprinkled on it to encourage the chicks to take the seed. Secure a low perch in the cage about the fourth day. Once the chicks are steady on this, add a second, higher perch.

Youngsters differ in how quickly they convert to a dry-seed diet. Some chicks sit and wail to be fed; never attempt to place them back with their parents. Wipe some softfood on their beaks to entice them to eat. After feeding, gently wipe their beaks, as hardened food causes sores. By six to

Seventeen-day-old fledglings about ready to leave home. Photo by Ron Moat.

eight weeks of age the chicks should be fully weaned. Offer little, if any, greenfood during weaning, as this may prompt diarrhea. Greenfood can be safely introduced once the chicks are on a dry-seed diet. As the chicks cope with the dry seed, reduce the softfood. The transition from one diet to another should be smooth.

RINGING

Chicks should be permanently identified with leg bands, also called rings. If you sell your birds to a pet shop, the only way a dealer will know your birds at a later date is by their bands. In addition, it is sometimes not possible to enter unbanded canaries in an exhibition.

Rings can be ordered through your specialty

canary association. Many breeders have bands specially made for their birds with their initials, code number and year on them. As a ring is put into use, record it in an index file. All pertinent information should be written down.

There are two ways to ring canaries. One is to use split rings. These are easily slipped onto the young when they are weaned from their parents. These are light-weight, colored plastic rings

A gorgeous Fife Fancy canary, wearing a plastic identification ring. Photo by Michael Gilroy.

that are consecutively numbered. Opened by a special tool, they are placed on the chick's leg.

The other method is to use closed rings. These must be put on the birds when they are six or seven days old. Bands placed on too early fall off. If the chicks are too large, the band will not slide over the foot. To place the ring, take the canary's foot between your fingers. The back toe should point towards the back while the other toes stretch towards the front. Greasing the foot with oil or petroleum jelly allows the ring to slip on more readily. Simply bring the front toes together and pass the ring over them. Then pass the ring over the ball of the foot and onto the shank of the leg until clear of the rear toe. Wipe the lubricant off with a soft, dry cloth. Thereafter, check that the ring does not become clogged with food or feces.

THE MOLT

Birds typically molt in July. The entire process should be complete by September, taking about ten to twelve weeks in all. The key to quick molting is to leave the birds alone in peace and quiet.

Provide them with regular bathing facilities and give them no cause for distress. The molt takes much energy from the birds, so everything should be more calm than usual.

Remember that colorfed varieties should be receiving their coloring agent before the onset of the molt.

Genetics

The object of breeding is to produce successively superior generations. It may seem simple enough to do this by purchasing top-quality birds and pairing only their best offspring. Should any faults appear, another good bird is found to correct the defect. However, the problem is that another fault may appear as the initial defect is corrected.

Obviously, merely purchasing quality stock and selecting the best offspring for breeding is not enough. First, faults must be recognized in the stock. Birds must be retained which do not exhibit these faults. In addition, birds about which little is known must not be introduced into the stud. Just because a bird looks good does not mean it is a good breeder. Inquire into its ancestry.

A full understanding of genetics is not crucial. Great breeders of the past produced good birds without understanding the complexities of the subject. However, in actuality they were utilizing the laws of heredity without understanding their mechanisms.

Through years of practical breeding, old timers knew that certain methods had to be used to obtain desired results. Today, our understanding of what is happening within the bird is of tremendous value. It saves years of wasted matings. An awareness of simple fundamentals explains so many problems. It enables us to appreciate just how difficult good breeding is. Additionally, the chances of producing reasonable stock increase with an understanding of genetics.

A duo of fledgling Gloster canaries. Photo by Horst Bielfeld.

CHROMOSOMES AND GENES

All animals inherit features from each parent. The means of doing so are via genes. Genes act as tiny units of information which tell the body cells how to develop. The genes are held together on bead-like structures known as chromosomes. There are many such chromosomes in all body cells. They are always in identical pairs, except in the sex cells.

Each canary receives one gene of each pair from each parent. It cannot receive two from one and none from the other. It is also pure chance which of the two genes of either parent it receives. If a normal green canary has two genes for green, it is pure for the color, or homozygous. Letters can be used to represent each gene. *GG* equals a pure green. The *GG* is the bird's genetic make-up, or genotype. If two such birds are paired together, the only possible gene color either parent could pass on is *G*.

The chicks are all *GG*, or green. The latter is termed their phenotype.

The next example considers one green parent and the other white. The green bird can only pass on a *G*, while the white can only pass on a White, or *w*, gene. The chicks would all be *Gw* in their genotype. But what is their phenotype? They will all be green—but it still carries the white factor. The combination can also be written as green/white. The color before the oblique line is visual; that behind it is present but not seen.

Genetic tinkering is behind the production of this exotic frilled Fiorino. Photo by Horst Bielfeld.

A green Gloster Fancy hen braces herself for the next round of stuffing her ever-hungry brood. Photo by Harry V. Lacey.

Such a bird is referred to as green-split-for-white. It is not pure for its genes, and it is therefore heterozygous, or impure for its color.

However, the Gw formula does not indicate that these two genes are the alternatives, or allelomorphs, of each other. This is important in more complex calculations. This is overcome by giving the mutated gene color a letter. In this case, w is for white. The alternative gene is given the same letter, but as a capital, providing it is the normal gene present in its unmutated form. Thus, the mating is better shown genetically as WW x ww = Ww, Ww, Ww, Ww.

The *Ww* is repeated four times because either of the *W* genes could combine with either of the *w* genes.

MATING SPLITS

The progeny of the green x white mating are known as the first filial generation (F1). If these are paired together, the next generation is known as the F2 generation, and so on. The original parents are the parental generation. Now we have a new situation to consider. If this F1 generation is cross paired, the birds are able to pass on either a gene for green or a gene for white. If the *W* gene combines with the *W* of the other parent, we have *WW*. If it combines with the *w*, we have *Ww*. Both appear to be green birds, but the former is homozygous, or pure for its color. The latter is hetero-zygous, or impure for its color. Likewise,

Above: A canary x siskin hybrid. These hybrids have little interest for most canary keepers. **Left:** An intensive yellow canary, showing smooth, dense feathering. Photos by Michael Gilroy.

the w of one bird can combine with the w of the other bird to give us ww birds—homozygous, or purebreeding whites. These are visually white because that is the only color present. In short, Ww x $Ww = WW, Ww, wW, ww$. One or two facts about genes can be established in light of our matings. First, genes do no mix to create intermediate states. Genes retain their individual identity. This was proved when we obtained pure white from the green/white birds. Next, certain colors (or features) can show themselves only when they are present in single dosage; these are dominants. Others must be present in double dosage before they are visual; these are recessives. Normally, the wild types of genes are dominant to later gene

mutations. In the examples given, the sex of the birds was unimportant. The calculations work out exactly the same if the cock or hen was green and the other white. Note that there are two types of green bird. One produces its own kind every time if mated to a similarly colored bird. The other produces some of its own kind and some which are different, depending on the genotype of its mate. Using this simple understanding of gene actions, we can understand how the mating of Crested Canaries to Non-crested works. The Crested bird is designated as Cc. The C stands for the crest gene; the c stands for non-crest, or Plainhead.
Pairing

the two results in *Cc* x *cc*. This can give only *Cc, Cc, cc, cc:* 50% Cresteds and 50% Plainheads.

Pairing two Plainheads, we get only 100% Plainheads. If we pair two Cresteds, in theory we would get 25% pure Crested, 50% Crested split for Plainhead and 25% pure Plainhead. Actually, the Crested is better in its heterozygous state because it is known that pure Cresteds are linked to a lethal gene. If present in double dose, the result is chicks that die in the shell or at young age. The gene for crest is an example where the mutant gene is dominant to the normal, wild-type gene.

MUTATION

A wild-type gene expresses itself in a predictable manner. If it is for green, it always remains a green. Periodically, and for no known reason, a gene suddenly changes in the manner of its expression. This is known as a mutation. Once the gene has mutated, it behaves as a normal gene. It is reliably predictable, unless the mutated gene was itself to mutate at a later date. If the mutation is considered of value to breeders, it is selectively bred for, in order to establish it.

However, when a gene mutates, it may have unseen effects on a bird, or it may be linked to an undesirable quality. In 99% of cases, mutational genes are actually unfavorable to the birds. Were we not to establish the mutations in our domesticated varieties, the normal wild state would rapidly return, since the majority of mutations are recessive to the wild-type genes.

Bright, colorful, and movable toys have high appeal to most cage birds. Photo by Michael Gilroy.

RANDOM SELECTION OF GENES

There are two phenotypes and three genotypes possible in the green/white x green/white mating. Whether or not any whites actually appear in a single clutch is

containing either the green or the white gene within them; the female likewise in her ova.

Over vast numbers, it is possible, when looked at in terms of two or three eggs, for chance to bring the whites together and so on. Over large numbers the calculations work out. The larger the number of matings and eggs, the more accurate is the theoretical expectation.

pure chance. The probability is one in four. Likewise, there is a three-in-four chance of producing a green bird and a one-in-four chance of a purebreeding bird. In a clutch of two eggs, both the chicks could be white, or they could be green. There may even be one of each. The reason is that genes are totally random in combining with one another. A male has millions of sperm

DEVELOPING A STRAIN

A big winner is not worthless. Indeed, if it was a chance happening in an otherwise ordinary stud, the breeder should hang onto the bird. Such good fortune does not come along that often. The value is such that a stud is normally greater than the price it may realize.

Assuming records have been kept, the breeder should check its pedigree to see if the parents came from a known strain. If so, I would return to that strain. A few sound hens with the star cock could be the basis for all future breeding. All other stock could be sold. If no strain was involved, I would purchase a good trio of hens from a single strain, or two trios from differing strains, where

both resembled the cock in many features.

From here on, no outside stock is introduced—at least for a few generations. Our understanding of genes tells us that bringing in other stock, regardless of its quality, means introducing many unknown factors. The

A fawn Border Fancy canary. A bird of this somber, wild-type coloration would likely have little appeal for most pet bird keepers. Photo by Michael Gilroy.

objective is to remove known faults and fix in known virtues.

The cock is mated to each hen. Only the very best youngsters are retained. The hens of differing strains are kept distinct so it can be seen which strain blends best with the cock. If both develop well, there is no need to bring in outcrosses. The two strains are probably unrelated enough to serve this purpose. With each new generation, progressively more is known about the breeding state.

Initially, close inbreeding is done to reveal faults in the genetic make-up of the stud. Thereafter, a program of linebreeding is followed. This is inbreeding on a more dilute basis. Understand that inbreeding itself does not create problems—it merely brings them to attention more quickly than normal. If the

desired features are *AA* and the parents are both *AA*, nothing changes that.

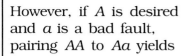

However, if *A* is desired and *a* is a bad fault, pairing *AA* to *Aa* yields 50% *Aa* and 50% *AA* progeny. Pairing the *Aa* with an *Aa* gives 25% *aa*. It is only by removing these that the stud becomes more pure for *A*. Since we do not know whether the retained birds are pure *AA* or heterozygous *Aa*, both looking the same, only over many generations can purity for the *A* feature be established.

In the example of a top winner, eight pairs of genes represented the overall bird. It can be appreciated how many permutations there can be between two birds. The reality is that the eight pairs of genes may control only a part of a bird. This means even more gene

In spite of the kaleidoscopic variety found in canaries, they are all variations on a central theme: *Serinus canaria,* the original wild canary. Photo by Michael Gilroy.

pairs control other features. The potential permutations are astronomical. This is why birds of such diverse quality are seen. Therefore, the approach is not to keep mixing genes, but to work on them a little at a time. A good eye for quality and an appreciation of the standard are as essential to a breeder as is the understanding of genetics.

ENVIRONMENT

Careful breeding gives a bird the genetic potential to develop to a given standard. A bird cannot be better than the quality of its gene

A variation on the red theme: an intensive red canary. Photo by Michael Gilroy.

potential, no matter how well it is kept and fed. However, a bird can fail to reach its potential if it is not managed and fed correctly. Such a bird can appear inferior to a canary of lesser genetic quality which has been brought to its full potential by an experienced breeder. It is essential to combine sound husbandry with a good eye for quality and understanding of the workings of genes to produce a good line

A dimorphic red factor hen. Photo by Harry V. Lacey.

of canaries. Each element is as important as the other.

FURTHER STUDY

This book does not discuss sex linkage, incomplete dominance, genetic variance, polygenic traits and other important aspects of breeding theory. Hopefully, stressing the basic points puts you in a better position to move on to these aspects. The interested reader should study books on genetics. It is not necessary that they relate particularly to canaries. The principles of heredity apply to all life forms. However, there is much not understood about the genetics of color and type in canaries. This is why detailed record keeping is vital.

Exhibition

There are few greater pleasures for a canary breeder than to see the results of planning and hard work recognized. Wins may be forgotten over the years, but that first award stays firmly fixed in the memory. There is a lot more, though, to exhibiting than simply breeding fine birds. Careful planning is needed. This begins before the show season commences. Indeed, it never stops. Even in the non-show season, cages must be prepared and birds trained.

A few of the colorful rewards of the bird show circuit. Photo by Donald Peret.

THE SHOW TEAM

The exhibition season runs from September through April in the UK and USA. The biggest shows are held from October to February. Each exhibitor decides well before the season of showing how many birds to include in the team. Do not attempt to show too many birds. This quickly becomes frustrating when some are not up to par on the show dates and replacements are unavailable.

Also, consider how many

A typical, compact show exhibition cage, complete with seed and water cups. Photo by Horst Bielfeld.

times to exhibit a bird in a season. This depends on the vigor of the stock, the temperament of the individual bird and its importance in the next breeding season. Birds shown too much during the winter are less likely to produce fertile eggs in the spring. They will not have had time to reach prime breeding condition.

SHOW TRAINING

The amount of show training a bird requires, to some degree, is determined by its variety. All varieties, though, need training. The birds must be steady and move with confidence from perch to perch. The judges must see them in their most favorable light.

Once an unflighted bird has completed its molt, a show cage is attached to its stock cage. Open the doors so that the youngster can hop to and fro between the cages.

Once the bird is familiar with the show cage, close him in it for an hour. Over the coming weeks it should spend more and more time in the show cage. Eventually the bird should spend an entire night in it.

The object of training is to duplicate the conditions under which the bird will be exhibited. The more familiar the bird is to unusual sights and sound, the better. This means that people wearing glasses or hats should not alarm them. Some visitors should be loud spoken, others should bend down to peer in the cage. Generally, do everything that happens at a show.

SHOW PREPARATION

Some breeders bathe their birds prior to each show. Others restrict their efforts to regular spraying. Stop bathing and spraying about two days before the show. This allows a bird's natural oils to give the feathers a

For many canary keepers, exhibiting is one of the most exciting aspects of the hobby.

final sparkle. Do not show a young bird for a minimum of three weeks after its molt is complete.

SHOW CAGES

Different canary varieties have their own special show-cage designs. The requirements are set by the governing body. The color of paints is quite specific. Likewise, any noticeable marks result in disqualification of your exhibit on the grounds of a "marked cage."

To assure everyone an equal chance, there is no way of knowing who owns which birds. The cages have a numbered label.

Be sure that your cages are spotless. Should your bird be equal to another, the general presentation of the exhibit and its cage may be the deciding factor.

EXHIBITION STATUS

Canary exhibitors are divided into two classes: novice and champion.

Unlike most livestock shows where the animal gets the status, it is the breeder who gains the status when showing birds. Persons entering their first show are novices. They remain so either for a fixed period of time or until they have gained a certain number of wins in open shows. Check the rules of your competition. Rules differ from area to area.

Once you are a champion, you remain that forever. Even if you drop out of the fancy and return after a few years, you are still a champion. A champion breeder commands more money for stock than does a novice. However, progress to the higher status is not without drawbacks. For example, the competition is much tougher for champions; wins are not gained so easily.

SHOW ENTRY

You must write to the secretary of the show and request a schedule in order to enter a show. The shows are advertised in avicultural magazines. Lists also are issued by specialist variety clubs.

The schedule indicates the various classes being staged. Fill in those in which you have birds to enter. Exercise care, as quite often people enter an incorrect class. When they return to their exhibition after judging, they find that they have been disqualified for being in the wrong class. It is sometimes difficult to decide exactly which class to enter—especially where marked birds are concerned. An experienced exhibitor is therefore a useful friend at this time.

When completing the entry form, fill in the section denoting specials on offer from the various clubs. Failure to do so could mean that another bird which yours had beaten in its class has its cage adorned with the club specials. Of course, you must be a paid member of the given clubs patronizing the show.

JUDGING

Judging is done behind closed doors in the UK. When it is complete, the public and exhibitors are allowed into the hall. The system may or may not be similar in other countries.

Accept the verdict graciously after judging, whether you have won or lost. If you did not receive a prize, study the winners. Discuss their merits with experienced breeders. Learn from defeat.

Diseases

Canaries suffer little in the way of ill health if they are given a sound diet and good, clean accommodations. It is well known by owners that these factors are the most likely to affect good health. There are times when a bird becomes ill through no fault of the owner. There are many ways, impossible to guard against, in which a disease can be

clean. If you keep more than two or three canaries, a hospital cage and an infrared lamp are essential.

A bird's posture can give clear indication as to its state of health. Photo by Michael Gilroy.

transmitted.

Prevention is always better than cure. Therefore, ensure that cages, aviaries and equipment are always

A reliable thermometer and a thermostatic regulator to control the lamp are ideal. Such equipment is not costly these days. In any case, they pay for themselves time and again in saving birds that might have died but for the controlled, warm environment.

The metabolic rate of birds is extremely fast. This means an ill bird can die in a matter of hours. Prompt action, though, often effects a rapid recovery. The first thing you must do is recognize

food. The eyes are not wide-awake bright. The droppings may be either very hard or very copious. Do not leave a bird in this condition overnight to see how it looks the next day.

ISOLATION
There are two occasions when a bird must be isolated from the rest of

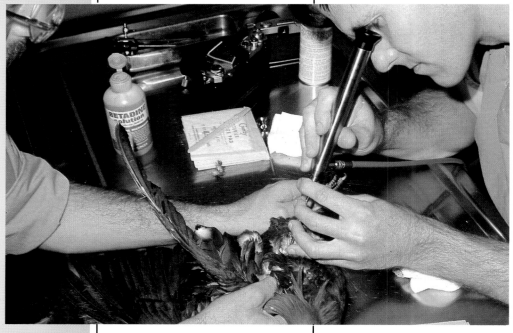

Diagnosing and treating bird diseases has greatly improved in recent years, due to advanced equipment and techniques. Photo by Wm. C. Satterfield.

an ill bird. The second thing is to isolate it immediately and apply heat.

THE SICK BIRD
An ill canary does not sit well on its perch; both feet grasp the perch, its feathers are fluffed out and its head droops. The bird shows little interest in anything, including its

the stock. The first is after the initial purchase. Regardless of how reputable the breeder or pet shop, a bird could be incubating a disease. Any new addition to your stock must be isolated for 21 days to ensure that it is not harboring an infection.

The second occasion of isolation regards a sick bird. The canary should be

transferred to a hospital cage with a temperature of 29.5–32°C (85–90°F). All food other than seed and water is discontinued. Medicines can be given via the drinking water; the higher temperature prompts the bird to drink more water. Consult a veterinarian if the problem worsens. Once the problem is cleared, the canary is acclimatized to its normal accommodation temperature over a few days.

Exhibition birds are constantly exposed to the risk of disease in the show environment. Infection can be transmitted via the show cage being in contact with so many others. Since few breeders keep their show teams separate from their main stock, the risk of contamination is likely. It is a wise precaution to separate your show team from your main stock, as the risk of contamination can be minimized.

THE PET BIRD

Pet canaries are less subject than show and aviary birds to risk of

An unfortunate canary afflicted with "tassle foot," a parasitic infestation.

An aerosol sprayer, or mister, comes in handy both for applying disinfectant and humidifying breeding cages as the chicks hatch. Photo by Mervin F. Roberts.

a fairly constant temperature to avoid this situation.

COMMON AILMENTS

The following ailments are those most commonly met. The potential list is, of course, extensive. Interested readers are advised to purchase a good reference book.

Air-Sac Mite A number of mites can invade the upper respiratory system. Signs are general loss of condition, sleepiness, partial or total voice loss and wheezing. Treatment should be under veterinary supervision. It is unlikely that a breeder would correctly diagnose the symptoms.

Constipation This may be induced by obesity, lack of fitness or excess fibrous material in the diet. The feces are overly dry and retained in the rectum. A few drops of cod-liver oil on the seed helps, as does the addition of greenfood to the diet.

Diarrhea Unduly copious feces indicate a problem in the digestive tract. The cause may be simply too much greenfood. Dirty feeding utensils also create the problem. Reduce the greenfood and sterilize the feeding containers. If the condition does not clear itself rapidly, consult your

ailments. This is because they live in a more protected environment. Nonetheless, high standards still must be maintained. Particular attention is given to the regular cleaning of a bird's cage—especially the floor tray.

Another potential problem in a home environment is created by central heating. Temperatures fluctuating wildly between night and day may induce a soft molt. Indeed, a bird may be in a virtually non-stop slow molt. It is best to maintain veterinarian. Diarrhea is often a symptom of other, more serious diseases.

Dead-in-Shell There are many reasons a chick dies in its shell. It may have contracted a disease when its shell was scratched and bacteria entered. If the egg was too dry, the chick may not have been able to cut itself free from the shell. Regular spraying of the parents helps to maintain humidity in the nest.

The hen may pass an infection to the chick while it is in the embryonic state. This kills the chick before it hatches. It is also possible that the chick had a hereditary condition which prevented

development. If dead-in-shell is a recurring problem in your stud, have your vet perform a post-mortem to establish the cause of death. Corrective measures then can be taken.

Egg Binding This has many causes. The most common is an incorrect diet at the time the egg was formed. A calcium deficiency results in a soft-shelled egg which the hen strains to release. If measures are not taken immediately, the hen may die from exertion. Hens unfit for breeding are another common cause of this problem. Ensure your stock is in top condition prior to the breeding season.

Feather Plucking Both cocks and hens may pluck their own or the feathers of other birds. The reasons may be lice, mites, stress, dietary deficiency, boredom or a

A canary suffering from alopecia of the head region. The cause is unknown.

hereditary factor. Once the habit forms, it is difficult if not impossible to cure. Separate the feather pluckers from the rest of the stock. Check for each potential cause. Never breed a bird with a history of feather plucking.

Going light This term indicates that a bird is loosing muscle—usually apparent around the chest and thighs. A dietary deficiency may be the cause, or it may be the result of some other disease process. Consult your veterinarian.

Lice and Mites These creatures are not respectful of immaculate bird rooms. Heavy infestations, though, are indicative of poor cleanliness. The northern fowl mite and the red mite are the two most typical parasites. The latter hides in the crevices of the cage or in the nest pans and boxes. It ventures out at night to feed on the blood of its host. The former are similar but attack the base of the feathers. Treatment of the bird alone may result in re-infestation. The cage and its apparatus must be treated with a suitable acaricide from your vet. All perches, nesting materials and the like must be burned and replaced.

Overgrown Beaks and Claws Overlong claws can be trimmed with sharp scissors. Be careful not to cut the "quick."

This is the blood supply visible when the claw is looked at carefully. The beak is trimmed in the same manner. If you are not confident about this, your veterinarian or a bird breeder can attend to it.

Index

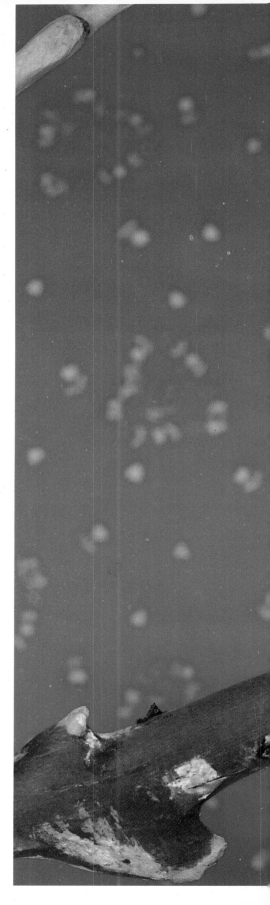